A Day in the Life of

INDIA

A Day in the Life of India WAS MADE POSSIBLE THROUGH THE GENEROUS ASSISTANCE OF:

DOORDARSHAN

**INDIAN EXPRESS
GROUP**

ADDITIONAL SUPPORT WAS PROVIDED BY:

MODILUFT

FUJIFILM

ATN

THE OBEROI GROUP OF HOTELS

VIMAL

The Taj Mahal at sunset.

S. PAUL

At the crack of dawn, a footballer shapes up for a big match at the Maidan Park grounds in Calcutta. Calcutta is rightly called the "Mecca of Indian soccer." Top players are often recognized and mobbed on the streets, and every match is followed with passion.

ARUN GANGULY

A Day in the Life of
INDIA

EDITOR AND SERIES DIRECTOR

David Cohen

EXECUTIVE DIRECTOR

Kirit Mehta

WRITTEN BY

Michael Tobias

PHOTOGRAPHY EDITOR

Raghu Rai

DESIGNED BY

Tom Morgan

CollinsPublishersSanFrancisco

A Division of HarperCollins*Publishers*

Buddhist monks pray at Sarnath on the outskirts of Varanasi. The Buddha came here to preach at Deer Park after his enlightenment. He told his listeners that life is filled with sorrow caused by ego and desire and that liberation could be achieved through the Eight-Fold Path: Right Understanding, Thought, Speech, Action, Life Style, Endeavor, Mindfulness, and Concentration.

RAGHU RAI

Early morning commuters travel between Sabalpur Diara village and Rani Ghat, in Patna. The Diara villages are spread over 12,355 square miles (32,000 square kilometers) of rich Ganga flood plains, and island dwellers who travel to Patna every day still rely on small boats and car ferries. Passengers pay as little as five rupees (17 cents) per crossing.

PRASHANT PANJIAR

Published in the USA by Collins Publishers
1160 Battery Street
San Francisco, CA 94111
HarperCollins Web Site: http://www.harpercollins.com

Originally published in a different form in India as *India 24 Hours®* in
conjunction with the film of the same name by CMM Ltd. by arrangement with
Grantha Corporation in association with Mapin Publishing Pvt. Ltd.
Text ©1996 CMM Ltd.
Photographs ©1996 by photographers credited.
India 24 Hours edition ©1996 CMM Ltd.
A Day in the Life of India edition ©1996 CPI.
A Day in the Life® is a registered trademark of HarperCollins Publishers. No use
of this trademark for books, calendars, films, or television programs can be
made without prior written consent of the publisher.

Library of Congress Cataloging-in-Publication Data
Tobias, Michael,
        [India 24 hours]
        A day in the life of India / text by Michael Tobias, photo editor
        Raghu Rai
                p.   cm.
        ISBN 0-00-225104-3
        1. India—Pictorial works. 2. India—Social life and customs—
Pictorial works. I. Rai, Raghu, 1942-   . II. Title.
DS480.853. 138   1996
954—dc20   96-33731
                                              CIP

Design by: Tom Morgan, Blue Design, San Francisco, California
Printed in China
10 9 8 7 6 5 4 3 2 1

Sunrise, in the countryside near Delhi.

S. PAUL

INTRODUCTION

Almost from the first days of photography, artists and filmmakers embraced India, recognizing it as one of the richest visual palettes on Earth. Early photography in the region was expeditionary in nature. When the peripatetic British photographer Samuel Bourne traveled through the subcontinent gathering material for his famous *Permanent Record of India* during the 1860s, he brought 50 glass plates, two cameras, a ten-foot high tent and two crates of chemicals. To trundle this cumbersome load, he required the assistance of 42 porters, without whom, it was noted in the British press, photography in India would not have been possible.

To Indian city dwellers photography seemed equally adventuresome, a window into a remote rural heartland they had never seen. Early Indian photographers returned to Bombay and Delhi with a bewildering array of exotic landscapes, cultures, faces, and wildlife, all cohabiting the same vast land. Lala (Raja) Deen Dayal commercialized the craft in his studios in Hyderabad and Bombay, and by 1880 he was successfully marketing photographic portraits to the well-to-do. At the same time, Dayal documented the plight of impoverished rural Indians. His "Types of Emaciation, Aurangabad," (1899–1900) was one of the first successful uses of social documentary photography.

More than one hundred years after Bourne and Dayal, *A Day in the Life of India* approaches its vast subject with the same sense of adventure. The Indian photographers who participated in this project traveled to the far corners of their country to show the world an India it rarely sees. Their goal was to create a visual time capsule of the world's largest democracy on its golden anniversary of statehood.

Unlike any other book in this series, which normally utilizes photographers from throughout the world, *A Day in the Life of India* was photographed solely by Indian photographers, who conducted their work over the course of several days instead of the usual single 24-hour period. But the subcontinent boasts some of the finest photographers on earth, and they brought to this project a particularly Indian sensibility. "Some of the eternal truths cannot be avoided," says the renowned photographer Raghu Rai, shooting among the ancient cremation ghats of Varanasi. "So many technological and societal changes have taken place, but I think the heart of India lives on, relatively unchanged, and that should be the essence of our book. India has its own pace, and we must try to understand that pace."

When you gaze upon these photographs, you will see an ancient nation that has become a modern technological power, a vast population that will soon overtake China's as the largest in history, and a vibrant, anarchic democracy on the eve of its 50th birthday. But beneath it all, there is something else. Among these images, we hope that you too will discover the ancient rhythms and eternal heart of India.

—*Michael Tobias*

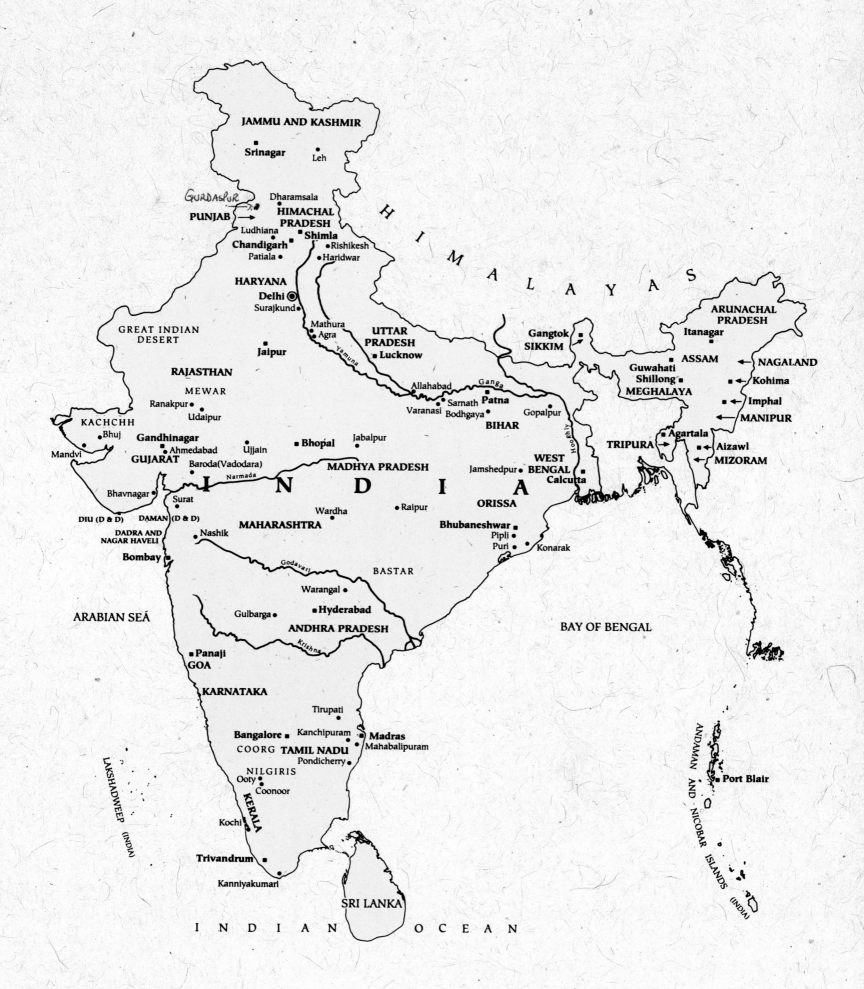

● PREVIOUS PAGES:

Morning at Sabzi Mandi, old Delhi's main wholesale vegetable market.

S. PAUL

● RIGHT:

At the Vinoba Bhave Ashram on the banks of the Dham River in the state of Maharashtra, one of 30 resident sisters spins yarn. The Ashram is run according to the ideals of Bhave, a follower of Mahatma Gandhi and the father of the Bhoodan or "land giving" movement. During the 1960s, Bhave's social experiments promoted village sustainability and independence through honest toil. The sisters living at this ashram grow their own food, weave cloth, pray, and teach Bhave's philosophy.

SWAPAN PAREKH

● **LEFT:**

Near the village of Burj Pawat in the Punjabi district of Ludhiana, gun-toting Bhairav Singh and his son Jasbir survey their fields. The Singhs successfully repelled three attacks by militants during Punjab's nightmarish years of terrorism in the 1980s.

YOG JOY

● **FOLLOWING PAGES:**

Somewhere between Warangal and Hyderabad in the state of Andhra Pradesh, a woman sorts through a red sea of chilies. Brought to Goa by Portuguese missionaries during the sixteenth century, chilies are among the most widely used ingredients in Indian cuisine. They are also used medicinally, allegedly to stimulate the heart.

JOHN ISAAC

● **LEFT:**

Awoman in Raghurajpur husks rice spread out for drying by repeatedly walking on it. On the wall is a drawing of Jagannath, a manifestation of Vishnu.

ASHVIN MEHTA

● **PREVIOUS PAGES:**

Fishermen mend their nets under billowing sails at Gopalpur in the eastern state of Orissa.

ASHVIN MEHTA

In Ahmedabad, the largest city in Gujarat, an elephant crosses a bridge over the Sabarmati river. Today, there are fewer than 8,000 wild elephants left in India.

RAJESH VORA

At the old port and cotton center of Bhavnagar in Gujarat, crushed salt is packed in polythene bags. Gujarat has long been associated with the manufacture of salt. One of Mahatma Gandhi's most famous protests was his march to the sea near the Gujarati town of Dandi where, in opposition to British law, his followers made their own salt. The Indian equivalent of America's Boston Tea Party, the march was a milestone in the country's long struggle for independence.

RAJESH VORA

Two Jain *sadhvis* or nuns, at the inauguration of a new *mandir* or temple in Baroda, Gujarat. In India today there are over 10,000 Jain monks and nuns who spend their lives walking from village to village promoting nonviolence, social activism, and empathy for all living beings. These two women are members of the white-robed Shvetambara sect.

JYOTI BHATT

● LEFT:

A Khatri Muslim block printer in the village of Tera near the Gujarati border town of Mandvi. Four million Muslims make up roughly 9 percent of Gujarat's population. The Mandvi area is famous for its traditional hand-printed and tie-dyed textiles.

JYOTI BHATT

● ABOVE:

Muslim women of the Jat community in Kutch, Gujarat, work for the private organization SHRUJAN, which employs more than 1,000 women. The various centers around the region teach traditional design and embroidery. The manufactured goods seen here will be sold in the city markets.

JYOTI BHATT

● **ABOVE:**

Mrs. Abdul Mara decorates an unfired earthenware pot in the village of Jambudi on Gujarat's Kutch peninsula. Potters in Kutch are heavily influenced by the Harappan culture, now in Pakistan. Though the potters are Muslims, they follow an ancient Hindu tradition whereby men fashion the pots and women do the decorative work.

JYOTI BHATT

● **ABOVE:**

A woman embroiders cloth in the village of Pipili, near Bhubaneshwar in Orissa. Local residents are acclaimed for their exquisite appliqué work on ceremonial umbrellas, cloth bags, quilts, and canopies.

ASHVIN MEHTA

● **LEFT:**

Kerala boatmen move their goods along a lotus-covered backwater fed by one of the state's 44 rivers. Kerala is home to Jews, Christians, Marxists, National Democrats, Socialist Republicans, Ezhava and Nair Hindus, and Union Muslims. A traditionally matriarchal society with a consistently Communist government, Kerala boasts the highest literacy and lowest fertility rate in India. Its labor force, however, tends to be overqualified and underemployed. This is largely due to strong labor unions, an effective land reform movement and high wages, which have discouraged outside investment.

NITIN RAI

● **FOLLOWING PAGES:**

These unsold marigolds from the wholesale flower market near Mullick Ghat were dumped in the Hooghly river near the Howrah Bridge in Calcutta. The 1,500-foot cantilever-type bridge was opened for traffic in 1943 and remains one of the busiest in the world.

ARUN GANGULY

● **ABOVE:**

A student prepares for her lesson at a government high school at Jharsently. Compared with much of India, the literacy rate is quite high in the state of Haryana—67 percent for males, 40 percent for females.

S. PAUL

● **PREVIOUS PAGES:**

A long the ghats of Mathura in Uttar Pradesh, women perform morning *puja* or prayer.

NITIN RAI

● **RIGHT:**

F ather and daughter in Gulbarga town in the state of Karnataka. Here, the tribal community is called Buru Buru Pocha. Members worship the Goddess "Durga," or "Durgamuru-gamma," as they call her. Durga, originally, known as Uma, was consort to the great god Shiva. As a manifestation of Kali, she retains aspects of a war goddess, but her images are invariably benign in spirit, conveying a sense of gentleness.

JOHN ISAAC

● **ABOVE:**

Mother and daughter enjoy an outing in Ned Chand's Rock Garden at Chandigarh, Punjab.

YOG JOY

● **LEFT:**

A mother with child in the Vyara District near the city of Surat in southern Gujarat.

RAJESH VORA

Students in Udaipur, Rajasthan, use traditional Indian school slates instead of paper. This is because paper is expensive and can only be used once. India's annual crop of 20 million newborns requires 127,000 new schools and 373,000 new teachers each year just to keep pace.

MAHENDRA SINH

At Breeks School in the Nilgiris, girls march to the playing fields to say the Lord's Prayer. This is a carryover from the days when Breeks, founded by the British in 1872, catered exclusively to European children. Now Breeks' 1,050 students are mostly local, and over half are from working-class Hindu Badaga families. Student fees are modest, only 160 rupees or $5.28 per month. Breeks is regarded as one of the best schools in southern India, with more than 90 percent of its students continuing on to university.

SAVITA KIRLOSKAR

Kerala boys queue to touch their guru's feet and receive his blessing. Traditional master-to-student education is one of India's great gifts to the world.

NITIN RAI

Porters at the Bhavnagar train station, Gujarat. For the last 50 years, female coolies of the Bhor tribe have pushed luggage trolleys in Gujarat. An estimated 11,000 trains carry close to nine million passengers everyday in India, but fewer trains now come to this region, and so the porters' income is slipping. They earn a mere eight to ten rupees (26 to 33 cents), on average, for eight to ten hours of hard labor.

RAJESH VORA

Punjabi policemen and women during an exercise. Noted for their exceptional skill with arms, some Punjabi police are also famed for their tradition of singing on the job.

YOG JOY

● **LEFT:**

Construction workers in Bombay churn out another highrise. Seven hundred new migrants arrive in the metropolis every day, and an estimated 76,000 new homes are needed each year. As a result, real estate prices have risen 1,000 percent in the past decade. Apartments in the Worli, Malabar Hill, and Nariman Point sections of the city may cost as much as one lakh (100,000 rupees or $3,300) per square foot, on par with Tokyo or Paris. None of this is good news for Bombay's six million poor or for the construction workers themselves, who still earn about a dollar a day.

HOSHI JAL

● **FOLLOWING PAGES:**

Two traditionally attired Santhal tribe members in Naga village in West Singhbum, Bihar.

PRASHANT PANJIAR

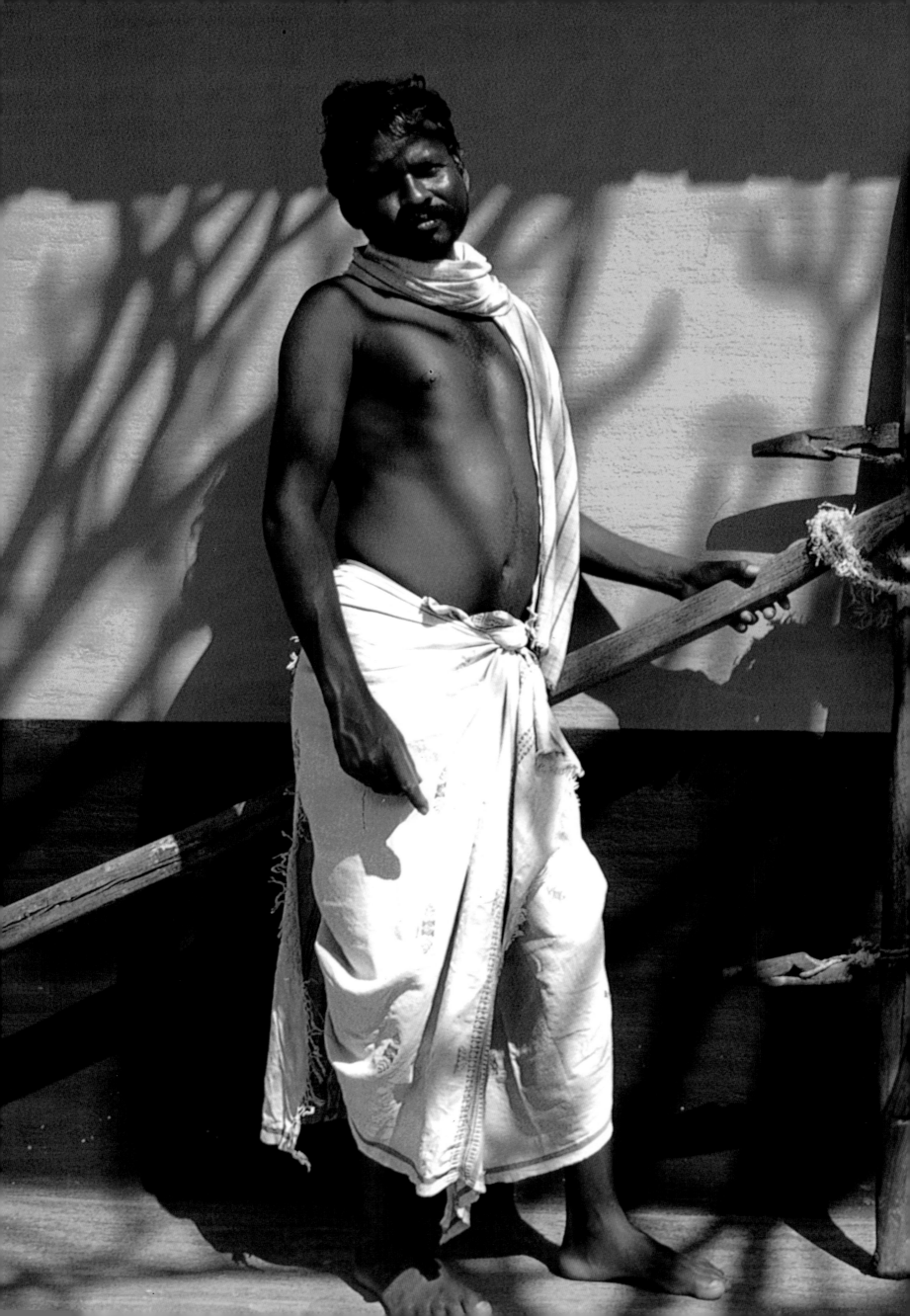

● **RIGHT:**

Curb-side buying and selling at the lively Ahmedabad stock exchange. There are similar exchanges in major cities throughout India. The largest is in Bombay.

RAJESH VORA

● **FOLLOWING PAGES:**

Kerala youths practice Kathakali face and body movements with their guru. It takes six to eight years to develop perfect muscular control of the finger, eye, eyebrow, face, neck, and body muscles. The performances are set to verses sung by musicians accompanied by drums and cymbals.

NITIN RAI

● **RIGHT:**

In Udaipur, Rajasthan, the Maharana Arvind Singh of Mewar reclines comfortably in the drawing room of his city palace. Singh descends from the royal family who ruled a large kingdom within what is now the state of Rajasthan. The titles and privileges of Indian princes were abolished by Indira Gandhi in 1971. Since that time, Mr. Singh has converted this Shiv Niwas Palace and the Fateh Prakash Palace, both in Udaipur, into five-star luxury hotels.

MAHENDRA SINH

● Rhino and egret at the Kaziranga National Park in the northeastern state of Assam. The one-horned rhino is the largest of the many rhino subspecies found in Asia and Africa. In recent years, its population has declined precipitously to fewer than 1,200. **NAMAS BHOJANI**

● A tiger relaxes in the lush forests of Kanha National Park, one of three such preserves in the state of Madhya Pradesh. Ecological pressure on the tiger's habitat is pressing from all sides, and tableaux such as this are becoming rarer each year. **RAGHU RAI**

Corbett National Park in the state of Uttar Pradesh. Here, in India's first national wildlife sanctuary, mahout Subedar Ali bathes his friend. Indian elephants are smaller than their African cousins and are further differentiated by smaller ears, four rather than three nails on each of their hind feet, and one rather than two lips at the tips of their trunks. Indian elephants are also more easily trainable, which has condemned many to lives of drudgery and indignity. Several years ago Ali was knocked off an elephant by a tiger who dragged him into the jungle and made off with a good portion of his scalp. **ADITYA PATANKAR**

● A majestic bull rests in Rajaji National Park in front of a Gujjar tribal hut. Here, in the Himalayan foothills, nomadic Gujjar cowherds have brought nearly 10,000 cattle into the park. The resultant overgrazing has damaged indigenous plant and animal species. India is home to half of the world's buffalo and 15 percent of all cows. Although more than 80 percent of Indians eat meat, both Hindu tradition and Indian law proscribe the slaughter and consumption of cattle. That, combined with shrinking pasture land, results in the starvation of millions of Indian cattle each year. **ADITYA PATANKAR**

The Punjab is India's richest farm belt. In 1993, the state produced twenty million tons of grain, one ton for each of the state's residents. Here, Punjabi sports enthusiasts engage in a bullock cart race at the Rural Sports Festival at Kila Raipur in the Ludhiana district.

YOG JOY

Every February, in the relatively wealthy agricultural state of Haryana, the traditional Surajkund *mela* is held. This colorful fair attracts tourists from nearby Delhi who come for handicrafts and traditional entertainment, including tightrope acts by members of the Baazigarh clan.

S. PAUL

A public demonstration of mind over matter at the Ludhiana district's Rural Sports Festival.

YOG JOY

● **LEFT:**

At the Aditi Pavilion of the Pragati Maidan exhibition grounds in New Delhi, a tribal dance by the Kalbelias, members of a snake-charmer community from Rajasthan.

S. PAUL

● **ABOVE:**

A traditionally adorned Rajput woman submits her application to the Self-Employed Women's Association. She signs with a thumb-print. The 50,000-member SEWA and organizations like it provide women with the means to obtain dignified employment and independent incomes.

RAJESH VORA

 TOP:

Cheerleaders employed by a tire manufacturer lend their support at a motorcycle rally near Madras.

AVINASH PASRICHA

ABOVE:

Water sports at Chowpatty Beach, Bombay.

HOSHI JAL

RIGHT:

In popularity, cricket is to India what baseball once was to America. Sachin Tendulkar, India's leading cricketer, recently signed a promotional deal that will net him $10 million, a fact not lost on these aspiring players in the heart of Bombay.

HOSHI JAL

● **RIGHT:**

In the Bastar district of southern Madhya Pradesh, Gond hunters perform a ritualistic Singh dance, a customary feature of a festival or marriage.

SWAPAN PAREKH

● **FOLLOWING PAGES:**

Sadhus, or holy men, dry their robes after a morning bath in the Ganga (Ganges). Like countless other pilgrims, they have come to take part in the Kumbh Mela, literally, the fair of the pitcher. The melas occur triannually, moving consecutively among four Indian cities—Haridwar, Nasik, Ujjain, and Allahabad, which is the most revered. The fourth mela, occurring every twelfth year, is always the most crowded with as many as 15 million pilgrims in attendance. The pitcher referred to is a primeval vase holding the nectar of immortality. In mythic times, the gods and demons struggled to possess this pitcher and four drops of nectar fell to earth in the four cities of the mela.

RAGHU RAI

A Varanasi businessman rushes past a meandering cow and its calf. Varanasi, like nearly all Indian cities, is jammed with cattle, which are revered in Hinduism and therefore allowed to wander freely. It is not uncommon for roving cows to bring India's busiest streets and highways to a complete halt.

RAGHU RAI

B uddhist monks gather in the ancient city of Sarnath, or Deer Park, where the Buddha preached his first sermon after enlightenment. It was here that Buddha founded the *Sangha,* the order of itinerant Buddhist monks. This morning, a large group of monks is receiving traveling money.

RAGHU RAI

● **LEFT:**

A wealthy Jain merchant, Rajesh Oswal, renounces the material world and becomes a monk before a community gathering in Surat, Gujarat. "Jain" derives from the word *Jina,* a term that means "conqueror" and refers to the conquest of all earthly desire. The founders were 24 enlightened preachers, known as *Tirthankaras,* because they succeeded in building a spiritual *tirtha* (a river ford in Sanskrit) across life's stream of rebirths and attained salvation. Only the last two *Tirthankaras,* Parsvanath and Mahavira, are regarded by modern scholars as historical figures. Mahavira, who created the Jain *sangh* or order, was a younger contemporary of the Buddha. The Jains believe in nonviolence—*ahimsa*—and the need for liberation from the karmic cycle of birth and rebirth by practicing "right faith, right knowledge, and right conduct."

RAJESH VORA

Near the famous Marble Rocks on the Narmada river outside Jabalpur in eastern Madhya Pradesh; two visiting picnickers enjoy the afternoon.

SWAPAN PAREKH

● **LEFT:**

An extended family of priests (*pujaris*), located between Cochin and Kerala's capital, Thiruvananthapuram. Extended families are one of India's oldest traditions, and it is not uncommon for four generations to live together under one roof.

NITIN RAI

● **FOLLOWING PAGES:**

Bombay's Chowpatty Beach on a hot winter afternoon. Chowpatty is the city's most famous seaside strand. Here, vendors sell *bhel puri* (popular snack food), *kulfi* (ice cream), and fresh coconut water, while a hardy few frolic in the water, risking high levels of pollution.

HOSHI JAL

● **RIGHT:**

Grooms gather at a mass marriage sponsored by the Punjab Police near Nurpur Bedi in Ropar district. At the wedding ceremony, couples will circumambulate the *Guru Granth Sahib*, the sacred Sikh book, four times, uttering four sacred sentences after each round. A sweet known as *deg* is distributed to all present and a sumptuous feast follows.

YOG JOY

A diamond cutting facility in Surat, Gujarat, a port located on the Tapti River, near the Gulf of Khambhat. Surat is noted for its chemicals and cloth, but is most celebrated for its precious stones, particularly diamonds. Here, diamond polishers await the verdict of supervisors who inspect their work.

RAJESH VORA

● **PREVIOUS PAGES:**

In the southern Rajasthani city of Udaipur, the driver of a three-wheeled taxi awaits a fare. Taxis are often decorated with auspicious symbols—flowers, posters, and little deities. In this case, the driver has chosen a poster of the late Divya Bharati, a 19-year old starlet who died mysteriously in 1993.

MAHENDRA SINH

● **RIGHT:**

In the historical town of Bhuj, Gujarat, two women approach a photo studio near the old palace grounds. The large portrait in the window is of Morari Bapu, a popular local narrator of the *Ramayana*.

JYOTI BHATT

● RIGHT:

The interior of the Jain temple at Ranakpur in Rajasthan. Set in the Aravalli range, the elegantly fashioned central temple is dedicated to Adinath, the first of 24 Jain *tirthankaras* or enlightened sages. Two other Jain temples here are devoted to the 22nd and 23rd *tirthankaras*, Neminath and Parsvanath. Built in 1439, the central temple's 29 halls are supported by 1,444 distinctly carved pillars.

MAHENDRA SINH

● FOLLOWING PAGES:

Fishermen empty their nets at Gopalpur beach near Konarak on India's eastern coast in the state of Orissa. Like nearly all of India's coastlines, this stretch on the Bay of Bengal has been overfished. Numerous species of fish, as well as the Olive Ridley turtle, have been brought to the brink of extinction, and only 19.3 square miles (5,000 hectares) of mangrove swamp remain.

ASHVIN MEHTA

● RIGHT:

A Toda woman in the village of Toror greets a male friend in the traditional manner: the man touches his bare foot to her head. Toda shawls, called *putxuty*, are normally embellished in red and black and fitted with pockets.

SAVITA KIRLOSKAR

● **ABOVE:**

Arunachal Pradesh, with its 82 distinct tribal groups, has some of the most remarkable tribal practices and magnificent scenery on earth. Here, a Nishi tribeswoman affectionately embraces a friend during a wedding ceremony. This Tibetan border state in Northeast India has fewer than 900,000 residents and a per capita income of less than $150 per year. Nearly 90 percent of the population still live in an aboriginal state, including the Sulung tribespeople, some of whom are said to dwell in trees, and at least one group of which is rumored to have no knowledge of fire. The old customs are likely to change, however, as even here, nearly 50 percent of the population has access to television.

NAMAS BHOJANI

● **RIGHT:**

Nishi tribesmen in traditional garb, including headpieces, swords, spears, and knives. The entire northeast region of India, including Arunachal (formerly the Northeast Frontier Agency), Nagaland, Manipur, Mizoram, and Tripura, comprise one of the more remote regions in the world. Despite their relative isolation, the tribes of Arunachal have begun to encounter problems associated with modernization. New roads, expanding towns, and industrial development have depleted primary forests, destroyed watersheds, and threatened traditional tribal practice.

NAMAS BHOJANI

● **RIGHT:**

In the Gujarati Kutch village of Dhaneti, an Ahir farmer rests in front of her home. Her tattoo marks are traditional ornamentation that almost all women, even young girls, wear. The subtle variations in the motifs are associated with various agricultural and pastoral communities in the Kutch and Saurashtra regions of Gujarat.

JYOTI BHATT

● **LEFT:**

Meherangarh Fort is one of many splendid fortresses in Rajasthan. Built in the early nineteenth century by Maharaja Man Singh, it is now a palace museum operated by the former Maharaja of Jodhpur.

MAHENDRA SINH

● **FOLLOWING PAGES:**

In Madras, model Sindhu Suresh Tantri, decked out in temple jewelry normally worn by dancers, poses before a vintage 1930 Austin 12.

AVINASH PASRICHA

These two boys on Patna-Gaya Road are making their way toward the small town of Bodhgaya, the most important Buddhist pilgrimage site in India.

PRASHANT PANJIAR

Textiles—woven, printed, painted, brocaded, tie-dyed, stained, hand-colored, mirrored and beaded, spun and embroidered—are one of India's primary industries. In Ahmedabad, a Rajasthani immigrant named Kaluji dries printed cotton cloth on an improvised bamboo structure in a process house. Using a technique known as mercerization, color is stabilized and luster added.

RAJESH VORA

● **ABOVE:**

On the road to the annual Baneshwar Festival near the city of Dungarpur, a Bhil boy sells decorated scarves. The Bhil, along with the Minas and Bishnoi, are among the three major tribal groups in Rajasthan. Originally gatherers, the Bhils have, for the most part, taken up small-scale agriculture or moved into towns. For four days each year, large numbers congregate at Baneshwar for traditional singing and dancing in honor of their god Vaghdeo.

MAHENDRA SINH

A carpet vendor in old Delhi. In the background is the Red Fort, completed in 1648 under the reign of Shah Jahan. During India's long struggle for independence, the Red Fort took on symbolic importance, and it was here at midnight, August 14, 1947, that the British Union Jack was lowered and the Indian tricolor raised proudly towards the sky.

S. PAUL

● **FOLLOWING PAGES:**

A graceful gathering of women with their colorful *dupattas* or veils at performance of the Bhangra and the Gidda, traditional folk dances of Punjab.

YOG JOY

● **ABOVE:**

A *sadhu,* or holy man, stands one-legged in the courtyard of an ornate Mathura temple. For Hindus, penance is the basis of enlightenment. According to Vedic literature, the more affliction and austerity a body withstands, the closer the soul move toward *moksha* or emancipation.

NITIN RAI

● **RIGHT:**

A *sadhu* meditates on the banks of the Sangam, a place of renowned power where the Jamuna and Ganga rivers meet. The holy man is cloaked in the traditional saffron robe, and the markings on his forehead indicate that he is a follower of Vishnu. *Sadhus* often wander through India for years, and many make the arduous trek from the southern tip of the subcontinent to Mount Kailash in the Tibetan Himalayas at least once during their lives. Ultimately, the ascetic renounces all worldly attachments, wearing a loincloth or going naked altogether. Their goal is *moksha,* or release, from the ceaseless cycle of reincarnation.

RAGHU RAI

A live exhibition at the National Handloom and Handicraft Museum in New Delhi. Designed by well-known Indian architect Charles Correa, the museum is on the Pragati Maidan exhibition grounds.

S. PAUL

A young resident of Himachal Pradesh with a transistor radio. In a country where the radio was, until recently, the primary source of information and entertainment, a farm boy's first radio is still a big event.

ADITYA PATANKAR

M en lounge outside a house in Rajasthan. Houses throughout the state use local materials—mud brick, cow dung, and plaster—beautifully decorated with broken mirrors. Like the indigenous architecture of the Southwestern United States, edges are rounded and softened, courtyards are well-proportioned, and walls are thick to moderate temperature fluctuations.

MAHENDRA SINH

● ABOVE:

Badaga bride in the hills above Coonoor in the southern state of Tamil Nadu. All Hindu marriages are consecrated by the *pheras* or seven rounds the couple makes around a sacred fire. Hindu weddings also include pranks. The most common involves the bride's friends hiding the groom's shoes and demanding ransom for their return. A final *geet* or song, known as the *bidaai* or farewell, marks the daughter's passage from her childhood home to her husband's.

SAVITA KIRLOSKAR

● RIGHT:

Kodava wedding in the Coorg region of Karnataka. The Kodava, who have always refused to accept the Hindu caste system, are a community with a fierce sense of independence. Kodava weddings are conducted according to oral tradition. Usually, separate ceremonies are performed in the houses of the bride and groom. Here, at a third ceremony, known as *dampathi muhurtham*, guests pay tribute to the couple and offer gifts of money. The Kodava's significant wealth derives from land rich in rice, sandalwood, rubber, pepper, coffee, and spices.

JOHN ISAAC

● ABOVE:

A movie poster painter or "film hoarder" in Bombay. Movie hoardings, or billboards, have an epic sensibility—a passion for melodrama, grand gestures, and glaring colors. They are also in great demand since India has 12,000 movie theaters and 60,000 video stores. With 1,000 new films each year, India is the world's most prolific film producer.

HOSHI JAL

● RIGHT:

Bhagwan Basappa, who migrated from his village in the state of Karnataka, is a painter at Bombay's renowned Ellora Arts Company, one of the oldest movie hoarders in India.

HOSHI JAL

In Varanasi, a proud sculptor poses with his latest creation, a seven-foot statue of one of Varanasi's famed *akhara* wrestlers.

RAGHU RAI

● **ABOVE:**

A man made up as Hanuman, the Monkey God, seeks alms from passersby on the highway to Tirupati in Andhra Pradesh. Hanuman was an ardent devotee of Lord Rama. With an armada of monkeys, he helped rescue Rama's wife, Sita, from the clutches of the demon Ravana.

AVINASH PASRICHA

● **RIGHT:**

A colorful window in the Swaminarayan Temple in Bhuj, Gujarat. Depicted here are Krishna, Matsya, and Vaman, all *avatars* (incarnations) of Vishnu. Called "the Preserver," Vishnu is the second member of the Hindu trinity or *Trimurti,* along with Brahma, "the Creator," and Shiva, "the Destroyer."

JYOTI BHATT

● **PREVIOUS PAGES:**

Many Hindus believe that dying in Varanasi insures access to heaven. So, for 2,000 years, there has always been at least one cremation fire burning along the *ghats* of Varanasi, also known as Benares or Kashi. The pall of smoke leaves a durable haze over one of the world's oldest cities.

RAGHU RAI

● **LEFT:**

A lordly Brahmin bull stands above the Ganga near the cremation ghats of Varanasi. Here souls are jettisoned into the next life, dispatched as ash into the river. The Ganga meanders over 1,550 miles (2,495 kilometers) from its sacred aperture in an arching glacier at Gangotri to the steamy Bay of Bengal.

RAGHU RAI

● **RIGHT:**

Coal pickers at a steel and coal dump in Jamshedpur in the state of Bihar. Contractors bid for the right to recover bits of coal from this wasteland and employ women and children to do the dirty, backbreaking work. Since there is always a market for cheap labor and poor families need their children's wages just to subsist, India's child labor laws are often flagrantly ignored. As a result, there are more than 115 million school-age children in the Indian work force. This is a source of concern to human rights advocates both within India and internationally.

PRASHANT PANJIAR

● **FOLLOWING PAGES:**

The vast Markha range of the Ladakh Himalayas is punctuated by Mashiro Kangri (24,728 feet or 7,537 meters), Konglacha Peak (21,982 feet or 6,700 meters), and Stok Kangri (20,177 feet or 6,150 meters). These summits, sacred to Buddhists, are also prominent in Hindu literature as the nuptial seat of the god Shiva and his consort Parvati. Many ascetics still perform *yatra* or holy pilgrimage to the Himalayas, crawling on all fours for up to two months with only goatskin wrapped around their palms and kneecaps.

NOSHIR DESAI

● LEFT:

Village women in the Thar desert near the Pakistani border collect water from a bore well. Rainfall in this part of India averages fewer than ten inches per year, so desert dwellers have found ingenious ways to preserve water. The Rajasthani Bishnoi, for example, harvest dew drops from desert shrubs in the early mornings. They also monitor their animals to prevent over-forage and maintain cisterns against cyclical droughts.

MAHENDRA SINH

Traditional mud dwellings and thatched-roof huts in the village of Duv in Rajasthan's Thar desert. These traditional structures are ecologically sound and economically sustainable. Using indigenous materials, they are cool in the summer and can be heated inexpensively in the winter.

MAHENDRA SINH

● **RIGHT:**

The courtyard of a small mosque in Dhordo village in the Banni area of Kutch. Banni has many Muslim cattle breeders, and during the holy month of Ramadan, they observe a *roja* or fast. From dawn until dusk they are supposed to refrain from eating, drinking, or even swallowing their own saliva. In a region as hot and dry as the Kutch, the safest way to practice such discipline is complete inactivity. Here, a man reclines beneath a traditional *ajarakh* that cattle breeders also wear as a skirt.

JYOTI BHATT

● **FOLLOWING PAGES:**

At winter twilight, a Kashmiri lad named Farhad stands in a boat on Dal Lake. Surrounded by high peaks and sacred hills and ruins, Dal Lake is actually a maze of smaller lakes and tree-lined canals. For centuries these watercourses have been rhapsodized as the Venice of Asia.

NOSHIR DESAI

● LEFT:

In the Bastar district of southern Madhya Pradesh, a Gond hunter swims in a natural pool. Of the five distinct Gond groups, four practice hoe cultivation in two hilly regions—the Satpura plateau and the Chhattisgarh Plain between Ranchi and Bundel-khand. Members of the fifth group, such as this man, are traditional hunter-gatherers. Gond hunters are organized in patriarchal family systems, live in comfortable huts, and speak dialects of the Aryan and Dravidian language groups. They are said to be among the first inhabitants of India.

SWAPAN PAREKH

● **ABOVE:**

Guru Hanuman's *akhara* or wrestling school at Kamala Nagar, Delhi. Once the home of traditional sandpit wrestling, *akharas* these days use mats and astroturf. This *akhara* was opened in 1928 by Guru Hanuman, 95, seen here wearing a black coat and hat. The guru has trained more than 100,000 young athletes, many of whom have gone on to win major tournaments at the Asian Games, Commonwealth Games, and even the Olympics.

S. PAUL

● **ABOVE:**

Akhara wrestlers display their exuberant style on the banks of the Ganga in Varanasi, Uttar Pradesh.

RAGHU RAI

● **FOLLOWING PAGES:**

Near the Bhajan Ashram in the famous temple city of Mathura, Uttar Pradesh, is the answer to the old Indian riddle: At what stage in life do men and women cast three-legged shadows?

NITIN RAI

● **RIGHT:**

Cantilevered fishing nets such as these near Fort Cochin, Kerala, were introduced to India by traders from the court of Kublai Khan.

NITIN RAI

● **LEFT:**

The river Kosi flows through Corbett National Park, in the Himalayan foothills of Uttar Pradesh. India's first national park was named after Jim Corbett, a British hunter who was instrumental in its establishment. It was here that Project Tiger was launched in the early 1970s with money from the World Wildlife Fund (WWF). At the time there were fewer than 1,800 tigers in India, down from an estimated 50,000 at the turn of the century. Today the number may be as low as 1,000.

ADITYA PATANKAR

● RIGHT:

The city of Udaipur on the shores of Lake Pichola. The magnificent building in the center of the picture is the Shiv Niwas Palace. Now a hotel, it still houses the resident Maharana.

MAHENDRA SINH

At sunset in Varanasi, a man plays his flute to Goddess Ganga. Traditionally, the great Mother River was said to flow from the toe of Lord Vishnu. Despite the fact that it is among the world's most polluted rivers, the sacred water is believed to purify the soul and wash away the sins of those who drink it.

RAGHU RAI

The Taj Mahal at sunset. Constructed over a 22-year period in the seventeenth century, the Taj Mahal was commissioned by Moghul emperor Shah Jahan as a mausoleum for his beloved wife Arjumand Banu Begum, also known as Mumtaz Mahal or "the chosen one of the palace." Though it is India's most famous symbol, the architecture of the Taj is actually a mixture of styles from India, Persia, and Central Asia.

S. PAUL

● **LEFT:**

T he Victoria Memorial in
Calcutta was the vision of Lord
George Nathaniel Curzon, who was
appointed the Governor-General of India
in 1899. The Memorial was opened in
1921 and houses an art museum.

ARUN GANGULY

● **ABOVE AND RIGHT:**

Painters and their admirers gather at the opening of the "River of Art" exhibition at the Art Today gallery in Delhi. One work from each of India's greatest contemporary painters was selected for the show. In recent years, investing in contemporary paintings has become fashionable among Indian socialites.

S. PAUL

● **ABOVE:**

Nine-year-old Chenzung Chamba Norphel, a novitiate lama, passes the 50-foot copper and bronze Buddha image at Thikse Monastery in Ladakh. Thikse is a center of the Gelugpa sect of Tibetan Buddhism, a reform group founded by the first Dalai Lama in the fifteenth century. The four sects of Tibetan Buddhism—Nyingmapa, Kargyupa, Saskyapa, and Gelugpa—form part of the *Mahayana*, or middle path of Buddhism, with 155 million followers worldwide. Many Tibetan Buddhists found refuge in India after their homeland was seized by the Chinese in the 1950s. The Dalai Lama himself went into exile in 1959 and set up his temporal and spiritual authority in Dharamsala in the lower Indian Himalayas.

Although Buddhism originated in India and the Buddha (Lord Sakyamuni Gautama) lived and taught in India, only about 1 percent of Indians consider themselves followers.

NOSHIR DESAI

● **RIGHT:**

Leather shadow puppetry, which originated in India and spread throughout Southeast Asia, is now a dying art here. Nevertheless, residents of this rural village on the outskirts of Hyderabad have worked all day to prepare a firelit romance that holds the entire village in thrall. The hand puppets are cut from leather and elaborately dyed to cast a "colored shadow." Oil lamps are placed behind the screen to effect the shadow play. The puppeteers are staging a scene from the *Ramayana*, India's great epic.

JOHN ISAAC

● **ABOVE:**

The Law Garden in Ahmedabad opposite the city's law college was once one of the most secluded parks in the city. Students searching for a bit of privacy renamed it the Love Garden. More recently, the park's craft merchants and food vendors have attracted locals and tourists alike, but moments of quiet romance can still be found.

RAJESH VORA

On a festive evening in Varanasi, a boy tends a magnificent gilded carriage. Janmashtami is an all-India celebration in honor of Lord Krishna's birth. Depending upon astrological signs, the length of the festival varies from year to year, and state to state. During Janmashtami festivities, carriages are decorated, houses are cleaned, and cribs are adorned with dolls, sweets, and various toys for baby Krishna.

RAGHU RAI

● **ABOVE:**

Bombay's Suneeta Rao applies makeup at the Royal Western India Turf Club. She is preparing for a fashion show and concert held the day before the annual Derby. Rao, with two platinum albums, has merged artistry and business sense. She is not only trained in classical Indian dance and song but holds a degree in economics from St. Xavier's College in Bombay and the Bombay International School.

HOSHI JAL

● **RIGHT:**

Police women of the cultural wing of the Punjab police force get ready for an evening of entertainment in Patiala.

YOG JOY

● **RIGHT:**

Models take to the runway in a fashion show at the Royal Western India Turf Club in Bombay. Long one of the world's leading textile producers, India is now emerging as an important international fashion center.

HOSHI JAL

● **FOLLOWING PAGES:**

The lamplighter at the famous Vishala open-air restaurant in Ahmedabad, a hot spot for traditional Gujarati cuisine. Diners, who sit on the floor, are entertained by puppet shows and local dances.

RAJESH VORA

A Day In the Life of India Project Staff

EDITOR AND SERIES DIRECTOR

David Cohen

PROJECT MANAGER

Jain Lemos

DESIGN

Brenda Eno and Tom Morgan at Blue Design

FINANCE DIRECTOR

Devyani Kamdar

DEVELOPMENT DIRECTOR

Mira Kamdar

RESEARCH CONSULTANT

Shampa Banerjee Srivastava

COPY EDITOR

Lynn Ferar

ATTORNEY

Philip Feldman

A boy loads his bicycle with coconuts near Jagannath Temple, Puri. Except for the northern coast of Gujarat, coconuts and bananas grow in abundance along the entire coastline of India. **ASHVIN MEHTA**

India 24 Hours Project Staff

EXECUTIVE DIRECTOR

Kirit Mehta

PROJECT DIRECTOR AND WRITER

Michael Tobias

PHOTO EDITOR

Raghu Rai

PROJECT SUPERVISOR

Parul Shah

PROJECT COORDINATOR

Tasneem Neemuchwala

PHOTOGRAPHIC RESEARCH ASSISTANT

Mahesh Shah

RESEARCHERS

Meena Menon
Deepa Bhatia
Meenu Rajak
Kaumudi Marathe
Sameera Khan
Vasudha Gore

EDITORIAL CONSULTANT

Suchitha Shrinagesh

DESIGN

Paulomi Shah, Mapin Design Studio

Members of the famous Chandralekha Dance Troupe practice on Elliot beach in Madras. They are rehearsing for their forthcoming production of *Mahakaal*, which the troupe has performed internationally.
AVINASH PASRICHA

The India 24 Hours Film

EXECUTIVE PRODUCER

Kirit Mehta

WRITER, DIRECTOR, AND PRODUCER

Michael Tobias

ORIGINAL MUSIC COMPOSED AND ARRANGED BY

Ilaiyaraja

CO-PRODUCER

Parul Shah

ASSOCIATE PRODUCER

Neena Mehta

EDITORS

Radha Chowdhari
Anand Dika

ON-LINE EDITORS

Gaurav Jain
Ajit Vahadane

ASSOCIATE FILM DIRECTORS

Charu Kamal Hazarika, Mallika Jalan and Suman Mukerjee, Ajit Jha and Mona Sinha, Nandan Kudhyadi, Sabyasachi Mohapatra, Himanshu Malhotra, Rajiv Mehrotra, P. N. Ramchandra, Abhijit Sheth, Sivan and Vanessa Smith.

MUSIC CONDUCTED BY

Uttam Singh

POST PRODUCTION SOUND SUPERVISOR

K. Sethuraman

PROJECT COORDINATORS

Rudabah Nanporia
Tasneem Neemuchwala

India 24 Hours® is a registered trademark.

PHOTOGRAPHERS' BIOGRAPHIES

JYOTI BHATT
Vadodara, Gujarat
Bhatt became a painter at the age of 16, a career he pursued for 20 years. He then became involved in photography, documenting the living traditions of folk and tribal arts. His photographs have been exhibited throughout the world, and honored with the Grand Prix at UNESCO's Asian and Pacific Photography Contest in Japan, a gold medal at the International Print Biennial in Italy, the National Award at Lalit Kala Akademi's Art Society Annual Show in Bombay, and an award from the World Photo Contest at Fotokina in Germany.

NAMAS BHOJANI
New Delhi
Currently the photo editor of Business Today, India's leading business magazine, Bhojani's interest in photography developed while he was a student at Sri Aurobindo International Centre of Education (SAICE) in Pondicherry from 1970 to 1982. This was a bilingual program in which the liberal arts were taught in English and the sciences in French. He then came to Bombay where he was Senior Photographer for *India Today* and *Bombay* magazine. His work has appeared in leading publications such as the *Times of India*, *Indian Express*, *Time*, *Newsweek,* and *AsiaWeek*.

NOSHIR DESAI
Bombay, Maharashtra
Desai's work has been exhibited in leading publications and archived in various prestigious collections in the United States, Europe, and Asia. Noshir blends his academic background in psychology and sociology with the medium of photography to achieve an in-depth visual documentary of India's various subcultures. His recent work has been published in the book Bombay—The Cities Within. He is currently working on several new book projects including *Zoroastrianism* and *Ladakh*. Noshir conducts workshops on several aspects of photography, and he is a member of Bazaar Photo Agency in Europe and the Forum of Contemporary Photographers in India.

ARUN GANGULY
Calcutta, West Bengal
Ganguly began his career in 1957 with a box camera. He joined the Photographic Association of Bengal in 1960, a premier institution devoted to promoting the art of photography. Since then, Ganguly's work has been widely exhibited and published in leading magazines around the globe.

JOHN ISAAC
New York, United States
From a tiny village near Madras, Isaac made his way to New York, and since 1978 has been a photographer for the United Nations. He has been recognized throughout his career for his ability to go beyond the dictates of journalism to reflect the universal bond of all people. Isaac has received awards from the U. N. Environment Program, from GRAPHIS as best outdoor photographer of the year, Kodak's professional showcase award, several Nikon awards, and awards from Fotokina. Six of his photographs of Namibia were selected to be postage stamps. His book on the Coorg region of India was recently published by Mapin.

HOSHI JAL
Bombay, Maharashtra
With a degree in chemistry and physics, Jal has been a journalist for the last 14 years. He began his career as a reporter with *The Daily* and *Free Press Journal* in Bombay. After becoming chief reporter at the *Free Press Journal* he joined *The Indian Post* as its chief photographer. Jal has been with the *Times of India* since 1988 as its photo editor.

YOG JOY
Chandigarh, Punjab
Born in a small district that is now a part of Pakistan, Joy lives in Punjab and is the chief photographer for The Tribune Group of Newspapers published from Chandigarh. He is the recipient of many awards including the National Press Award given by the Press Institute of India, All-India Press Photography Competition Award given by the Press Photographers' Association, Calcutta, as well as the UNICEF photo award. He is a medal winner in the World Photo Contest organized by UNESCO/ACCU, Japan. His published photographic work includes over 2,000 outstanding images in national and international newspapers, periodicals, books, and catalogues.

SAVITA KIRLOSKAR
Bombay, Maharashtra
Though she has a master's degree in chemistry, Kirloskar has excelled in the field of photography in India. Before joining her current position at Reuters, she was a photographer for the highly regarded newspaper, *The Independent*, and before that for the popular daily *Mid-Day*.

ASHVIN MEHTA
Tithal, Gujarat
With nearly 30 years of experience as a professional photographer, Mehta's work has been exhibited throughout the world as well as in his homeland. Many books of his work have been published on a variety of subjects including the *Coasts of India* and *100 Himalayan Flowers*. His work has been published in national and international publications, and he has been repeatedly profiled as one of India's leading contemporary photographers.

PRASHANT PANJIAR
New Delhi
A self-taught photographer, Panjiar began his career with his interest in the peasant movements in rural Bihar. Working as a photojournalist for *India Today*, Panjiar has witnessed many major historical events over the last decade. He was in Iraq, Kuwait, and Saudi Arabia for nearly three months covering the Gulf War in 1991. He was in Afghanistan after the Russian troops withdrew, and then in China during the aftermath of the Tiananmen massacre. He has been to Pakistan several times when Indo-Pakistani tensions were at their peak and in Punjab covering the effects of terrorism in the state. He is currently working as photo editor of *Outlook*, a weekly newsmagazine.

SWAPAN PAREKH
Bombay, Maharashtra
A student of photojournalism and documentary photography at the International Centre of Photography in New York, Parekh's work can be seen in leading international publications including *Life*, *Time*, *The London Independent*, and many others. He was awarded first prize in the Spot News Picture category at the 1994 World Press Photo in Amsterdam, the Award for Excellence in the Magazine News Picture category at the 1994 Pictures of the Year competition in Washington, DC, 2nd and 3rd prize, and Honorable Mention at the Nikon World Photo contest. His portfolios have been awarded prizes for two consecutive years (1993, 1994) in the "under 35" category in photography competitions held by the Alliance Française.

AVINASH PASRICHA
New Delhi
After graduating from college in economics, Pasricha took up the family profession of photography in the early 1950s. He joined the United States Information Service, and was the photo editor of their publication *Span* for 28 years. He is well known today for his photography of classical Indian dance and music. His work has been published in all of the major Indian publications as well as international ones like *National Geographic* and *Life*. Pasricha's photography has also appeared in a number of books and exhibits that have been acclaimed around the world.

ADITYA PATANKAR
New Delhi
Patankar's work can be seen in magazines and newspapers worldwide, including the *New York Times*, *Connoisseur*, *Vogue*, *Nippon Camera*, *Huigesnoot Magazine*, *Connoisseur's Asia*, *NZZ Folio*, and the leading dailies in England and Europe. Considered an expert on elephants, Patankar photographed the 1,000-kilometer journey by elephant for the number one bestseller, *Travels on My Elephant*, by British travel writer Mark Shand, and was the still photographer for the documentary "Queen of the Elephants" made for the Discovery Channel.

S. PAUL
Ghaziabad, Uttar Pradesh
Paul began his career in photography in 1951 with the German camera Zeiss Ikon Neitar. The following year, his first picture of the canal landscape, entitled "Tranquility" was published in the British photography magazine *Miniature Camera*. In 1954, Paul got his first 35-mm camera, the Leica IIIf Elmar, and became chief photographer for Indian Railways. His photographs have been published in India, Great Britain, the United States, Germany, Switzerland, the Netherlands, Belgium, and Japan. He has a number of books to his credit, and was awarded the Parishad Sanman award in 1993 by the Government of India.

NITIN RAI
New Delhi
Rai, a commercial photographer, is currently working as picture editor for *Sunday* magazine and has worked on book projects on Delhi and Rajasthan. He has done assignments for *The Tatler* of London. He is the winner of the 1993 Nikon award

RAGHU RAI
New Delhi
Rai has been amazing the photographic world for over thirty years with extraordinary images that are uniquely his own. Between 1975 and 1995, he won the Nikon Photo Contest International Award eleven times, and in 1993, he was honored as the Photographer of the Year in the United States. His major photo essays have appeared in various magazines and newspapers around the world, including *National Geographic*, *GEO*, *Life*, *Stern*, *Time*, and *The New York Times*. Twenty-five of his pictures are in the permanent collection of the Bibliotheque Nationale in Paris. His magnificent books include *Mother Teresa*, *Dreams of India*, *Indira Gandhi*, *The Sikhs*, *Taj Mahal*, *Calcutta*, and *Khajuraho*.

MAHENDRA SINH
Bombay, Maharashtra
Sinh's work has been published in major magazines around the world including *GEO*, *Time*, *Newsweek*, *The New York Times Magazine*, *The Sunday Times Magazine*, *Paris Match*, and *Stern*. One-man shows and group shows have taken his photographs to all parts of the globe—from Hamburg to Jodhpur. He is currently working on a book on the Thar desert of India.

and his picture of the Ayodhya Babri Masjid demolition was published on the cover of *Time* magazine.

AUTHOR—MICHAEL TOBIAS
Los Angeles, California
Tobias—author, filmmaker, ecologist, and historian—has written 21 books and written, directed, and produced more than 100 films including *India 24 Hours*, which complements this book. A former professor at Dartmouth College, his work has been published and/or broadcast in over 50 countries. Best known are his ten-hour dramatic miniseries and best-selling novel, *Voice of the Planet* and his 26-part television series and book, *A Parliament of Souls*. Other works include *Rage & Reason*, *A Naked Man*, *A Vision of Nature: Traces of the Original World*, *Antarctica: The Last Continent*, *A Day in the Life of Ireland*, *Black Tide*, *Ahimsa: Non-Violence*, *Life Force: The World of Jainism*, and *World War III: Population and the Biosphere at the End of the Millennium*. Together with his wife, the film producer Jane Morrison, Tobias founded JMT Productions, with offices in Los Angeles, London, Bombay, and New Delhi.

RAJESH VORA
Bombay, Maharashtra
With a degree in visual communication, specializing in photography, Vora is a photojournalist who pursues his own interests and freelances in the editorial, documentary, and corporate arenas. He is currently working on several projects: a documentation of the customs and rituals of the Jain monastic life; a visual study of faith, devotion, and joy among the folk-god worshippers of rural Maharashtra; the plight of child workers and the widows who, rejected and humiliated by society, have taken refuge at Brindaban serving the Lord Krishna.

INDIA 24 HOURS SPONSOR PROFILES

Doordarshan

Doordarshan, the Indian National Television Network, is one of the largest broadcasting organizations in the world. It has three national channels that are available both by ground and by satellite. Two other channels are available by satellite. In addition, there are nine regional language satellite channels and four more transponders that link the transmitters in the Hindi-speaking states of the country. Doordarshan also runs a movie club, an international channel that reaches over a hundred countries, and has an affiliation with CNN for news and current affairs programs.

More than an airline, Air-India is India's cultural ambassador to the world. Air-India's planes are a microcosm of India. The decor, the music, and the uniforms blend to create an Indian ambience and atmosphere.

Over the years, Air-India has established the largest corporate collection of contemporary and traditional art. These works are on display in Air-India's booking offices around the world. They serve as a constant reminder of the rich traditions in India's heritage.

INDIAN EXPRESS GROUP

Established in Madras in 1932, the Indian Express Group was founded by Ramesh Goenka to provide a unifying voice that would reach out to people during the struggle for India's independence.

Today, the Group has 19 publishing centers across the nation and 31 publications in seven languages. With the country's largest readership, the Group today plays a crusading role in the country's social, cultural, and corporate sphere. It is an endeavor that has become an enterprise.

ADDITIONAL SUPPORT WAS PROVIDED BY:

MODILUFT   FUJIFILM   ATN   The Oberoi Group of Hotels

MODILUFT   FUJIFILM   ATN   THE OBEROI GROUP OF HOTELS   VIMAL

SPECIAL THANKS

A DAY IN THE LIFE OF INDIA
EXTENDS SPECIAL THANKS TO:

Bharti and Bipin Bhayani
Susan Bloom
Craig Brooks
Subrata Chakravarty
Dilip Cherian
Michael Claes
Dan and Stacy Cohen
Kara, Willie, and Lucas Cohen
Norman and Hannah Cohen
Maura Carey Damacion
Namita Devidayal
Dipika Dayal
Siddharth Dube
Lois and Mark Eagleton
Ken Fund
Lesley D. Gray
Rasik and Panna Hemani
India Currents magazine
Tony Jesudasan
Anna Kamdar
Chitra and Vinu Kamdar
Devyani Kamdar
Dilip Kamdar
Prabhakar "Pete" Kamdar
Pravin Kamdar
Abha Dayal Kaul
Himmat and Padma Khara
Judi and Kartik Kilachand
Tanil Kilachand
Caroline Koff
Arvind Kumar
Linda Lamb
Lavina Melwani
Ken Milburn
Sandy Miller
Farhan Nakooda
Rasik and Rama Parekh
Samresh Parida
Roger and Roma Pereira
Ganeve Rajkotia
Ashok Ranganathan
Susan Reich
David Schneider
Aradhana Seth
Dr. Manu Seth
Husmuk Shah
Rajesh Shah
Malvika Singh
Vanessa Smith
Barry Sundermeier
Anuradha Teja
Dr. Jaskaran Teja
Paul Weiser
Susan Wels

INDIA 24 HOURS EXTENDS
SPECIAL THANKS TO:

During the course of two years, many
people have worked very hard to
bring *India 24 Hours* to life. We at
CMM realize that without the
support of our colleagues, friends,
and family, *India 24 Hours* would not
have been the success it is. We would
like to take this opportunity to
express our heartfelt thanks and
gratitude to the following people:

Chandulal H. Mehta
Nirmala C. Mehta
Lalit Shah
Madhu Shah
Yogesh C. Mehta
Suresh C. Mehta
Romi Mahajan
Paras Shah
Francis of the Heras Institute,
     St. Xavier's College, Bombay
Bipin Shah, Mapin Publishing Pvt.
     Ltd.
Mallika Sarabhai, Mapin Publishing
     Pvt. Ltd.
Martin D'Souza, *Bombay Times*
Meenakshi Shedde, *Bombay Times*
Alok Bajpai, The Explorers, Bombay

THE PHOTOGRAPHERS
EXTEND SPECIAL THANKS TO:

Bashir Ahmad
Tsering Angchok
S. Anwar
Maharana Arvind
Sushobha Barve
Protima Bedi
Chandra Bhan
Students of Bharata Kalanjali
Capt. Sanjay Bharga
BRO's Himank Personnel
Chandralekha and her students
Major Durga Das Bassi
Dhananjayan
Parvez Diwan
Tashi Dorjey
Dr. I. S. Gilada
Smt. & Shri Manoj Gohil
Maya and Sat Singh Gumanpura
Farhad Gāuni
Deepak Gurjar
Hotel Khangri
S. Janardhanan
Students and teachers of Kalakshetra
Alistair Kenneil
Komal Kothari
Tashi Lama
Thakur Manvendra
Meraj-ud-din
Syed Mirza
Mohideen
Prakash Naik
Chenzung Chamba Norphel
Oberoi Palm Beach Hotel
Orissa Tourism Development
     Corporation
Suresh Parekh
Santosh Pasricha
Singh Piplia
Fayaz Qabli

Rachna Productions
Rajesh Raj
Smt. and Shri M. Srinivasa Rao
Ramsinhji Rathod
Anita Ratnam
Singh Rohet
Shek Hudhandu Sahib
Ven. Geylong Samphel
Ravi and Shakti Sharma
Ravinder Sharma
D. Shroff
Shrujan Design and Training Centre
Sunayana Shukla
Harshvardhan Singh
Jagmohan Singh
Mewar Singh
Tata Steel Rural Development Society
Jethalal and Vimal Thakker
Staff and students at Thiksey Monastery
P. K. Tripathi
J. Vishwanathan
Tsering Wangchok
Tashi Yangzom

MEMBERS OF THE CMM
TEAM INCLUDE:

Mohammed Ahmed
Sanjay Anabhavne
Sameet Baadkar
Sandeep Bamnodkar
Kevaldas Bansod
Christophe Baudesson
Sanjay Bhalerao
Bharat Bhanushali
Rekha Charatkar
Haresh Chauhan
Vijay Chauhan
Alpana Chhel
Jyoti Chugani
Vishal Chugh
Lenin D'Souza
Yeshwant Deogharkar
Ravindra Deshmukh
Sandeep Deshpande
Ashok Devan
Felicia Fernandes
Francis Fernandes
Sandra Fernandes
Xavier Fernandes
Kiran Gahlaut
Divyesh Gandhi
Sachin Gawde
Malati Gupta
Shahul Hameed
Karen Hill
Rohini Indap
Jagat
Avinash Jagtap
Gaurav Jain
Mahavirprasad Jain
Preeti Jain
Wilson James
Suma Jayaram
Antony Jose

Chetan Juthani
Parag Juthani
Sandeep Kamble
Anand Kanan
Sanjay Kanojia
Ghazala Khan
Joharali Khan
Sachin Khangaonkar
Tanvir Koreishi
Alpesh Kothari
Pauline Kroese
Vinod Kudapkar
Ajit Kule
Amit Kulshresht
Sanjay Kumar
Benedicta Lobo
Puneet Makhija
Ajaz Maniar
Sunil Mayers
Dhanesh Meher
Astrid Mendes
Deepak Mohite
Atul Naik
Devaraj Nair
Priyadarshan Nair
Nirmala Narayan
Jyotsna Padhye
Deepak Pais
Anil Panchal
Vaibhav Parab
Govind Pawar
Clifford Pereira
Jewan Pillai
Sanjay Prasad
Rugmini Rajgopalan
Raj Mohan Rao
S.P. Rao
P.S. Rawat
Roslina Rodrigues
Ankit Sahu
Anil Shah
Chetan Shah
Deepak Shah
Rajendra Shah
Shyam Sharma
Yojana Sharma
Savita Shekawat
Veerendra Sherugar
Sheth Manish
Manohar Shindkar
Lakshmi, Mukesh, Meena, Anil,
     and Tara Shroff
Kersi Shroff
Sanjot Sonalkar
Manish Srivastava
Raman Sundareshwaran
Gajeshwar Surve
Nalini Suvarna
Tariq Syed
Manjiri Thombre
Mona Tulpule
Lianne Vaz
Ninad Vengurlekar
Baburam Yadav

BIBLIOGRAPHY

BOOKS

Alexander, Michael. *Delhi and Agra, A Traveler's Companion.* Great Britain STE Edmundsbury Press Ltd., 1987.

Banwari, translated by Vohra, Asha. *Pancavati: Indian Approaches to Environment.* New Delhi, Shri Vinaya Publications, 1992.

Baru, Theodre de W. M. Gen. Ed. *Sources of Indian Tradition.* Vol.1. New York, Columbia University Press, 1958.

Bedi, Ramesh and Rajesh. *Indian Wildlife.* New Delhi, Brijbasi Printers, 1984, reprinted 1989.

Bhattacharya, Haridas. *The Cultural Heritage of India,* 4 vols. Introduction by Bhagavan Das. Calcutta, The Ramakrishna Mission, The Institute of Culture, first 3 vols., 1937, 4th vol., 1956.

Brata, Shasti. *India: Labyrinths in the Lotus Land.* New York, William Morrow and Co., 1985.

Bumiller, Elizabeth. *May You Be the Mother of a Hundred Sons: A Journey Among the Women of India.* New Delhi, Penguin Books, 1991.

Chapple, Christopher Key. *Nonviolence to Animals, Earth and Self in Asian Traditions.* Albany, State University of New York Press, 1993.

Collins, Larry and Lapierre, Dominique. *Freedom at Midnight.* New York, Simon and Schuster, 1975.

Coomaraswamy, Anand K. *The Dance of Shiva,* Rev. Ed. New York, The Noonday Press, 1957.

Crowther, Geoff; Raj, Prakash A.; Wheeler, Tony; Finlay, Hugh; and Thomas, Bryn. *India: A Travel Survival Kit.* Hawthorn, Victoria, Australia, Lonely Planet Publications, 5th edition, 1993.

Darian, Stephen G. *The Ganges in Myth and History.* Honolulu, University Press of Hawaii, 1978.

Desai, Anita and Epstein, Mitch. *In Pursuit of India.* New York, Aperture / A New Images Book, 1987.

Durrams, Brian and Knox, Robert. *India Past into Present.* British Museum Publications Ltd., 1982.

Fürer Haimendorf, Christoph Von. *Tribes of India: The Struggle for Survival.* Berkeley and Los Angeles, University of California Press, 1982.

Fischer, Nora. *Mud, Mirror and Thread: Folk Traditions of Rural India.* Mapin Publishing Pvt. Ltd., Ahmedabad, in association with Museum of New Mexico Press, Santa Fe.

Karnad, Sunand V. *Textbook of Sociology.* Macmillan India Ltd., 1986.

Lapierre, Dominique. *The City of Joy* trans. by Spink, Kathryn. Garden City, New York, Doubleday and Company, 1985.

Mehta, Ved. *Portrait of India.* New York, Farrar, Strauss and Giroux, 1970.

—. *A Family Affair: India under Three Prime Ministers.* New York, Oxford University Press, 1982.

Merton, Thomas. Ed. *Gandhi on Non-Violence, A Selection from the Writings of Mahatma Gandhi.* New York, A New Directions Paperback, 1965.

Moorhouse, Geoffrey. *Calcutta.* New York, Harcourt Brace Jovanovich, 1971.

Murphy, Veronica and Crill, Rosemary. *Tie-Dyed Textiles of India, Tradition and Trade.* Victoria & Albert Museum in association with Mapin Publishing Pvt. Ltd., 1991.

Naipaul, V.S. *An Area of Darkness.* London, Andre Deutsch, Ltd., 1964.

—. *India: A Wounded Civilization.* New York, Alfred Knopf, 1977.

Narayan, R. K. *The Ramayana: A Shortened Modern Prose Version of the Indian Epic.* New York, Viking Press, 1972.

On this night at the Victoria Memorial in Calcutta, rows of colored chairs will be occupied by a stream of theater goers.

ARUN GANGULY

—. *The Mahabharata: A Shortened Modern Prose Version of the Indian Epic*. New York, Viking Press, 1978.

Newby, Eric. *Slowly Down the Ganges,* New York, Charles Scribner & Sons, 1966.

Pallo Itino, Massimo. Ed. in Chief. *Encyclopaedia of World Art*, Vol. VII. "Greek Art—Indian Art," "India," "India Farther," and "Indian Art." New York, McGraw-Hill Book Company, Inc., 1963.

Panadiker, V. A. *Dynamics of Population Growth: Implications for Environment and Quality of Life*. New Delhi, Centre for Policy Research, 1992.

Pye-Smith, Charlie. *In Search of Wild India*. New Delhi, UBS Publishers Distributors Ltd., 1993.

Rai, Raghu. *Delhi*. Text by Varma, Pavan K. New Delhi, Indus, an imprint of HarperCollins Publishers, 1994. See also: Rai. *Mother Teresa, The Sikhs, Indira Gandhi, Taj Mahal, India, Calcutta, Khajuraho* and *Tibet in Exile*.

Rosenblum, Naomi. *A World History of Photography*, New York, Abbeville Press, 1984.

Saksena, S. K. *Environmental Planning Policies and Programmes in India*. New Delhi, Shilpra Publications, 1993.

Shad, Abdur Rehman. *Do's and Don'ts of Islam*. Taj Publishers, 1988.

Sharma, Arvind. Ed. *Our Religions*. San Francisco, HarperCollins, 1993.

Sharma, Jagdish Saram. *India Encyclopaedia*. Vol. II. S. Chand and Company Ltd., 1981.

Silveria, D. M. *India Book 1994-95*. Goa, Classic Publishers Pvt. Ltd., 1994-95.

Sinclair, Toby. *Introduction to India*. Twin Age Ltd., Hong Kong, 1991.

Spear, Percival. *The Oxford History of Modern India, 1740-1975*. 2nd Ed. Oxford, Clarendon Press, 1965.

—. *A History of India*. Vol. II. Penguin Books, India, 1990.

Tikader, B. K. *Threatened Animals of India*. Calcutta, Zoological Survey of India, 1983.

Tobias, Michael. Ed. *Mountain People*. Norman, Oklahoma, University of Oklahoma Press, 1986.

—. Ed. *Life Force: The World of Jainism*. Berkeley, California, Asian Humanities Press, 1991.

—. *World War III: Population and the Biosphere at the End of the Millennium*. Sante Fe, Bear & Co., 1994.

Tully, Mark. *Defeat of a Congressman and Other Parables of Modern India*. New York, Alfred Knopf Publishers, 1992.

Tyler, Stephen A. *India: An Anthropological Perspective*. Rice University, Pacific Palisades, California, Goodyear Publishing Company, 1973.

Walker, Anthony R. *The Toda of South India*. Hindustan Publishing Corporation, 1986.

Wirsing, Robert and Nancy. *Ancient India and its Influence in Modern Times*. New York, Franklin Watts Inc., 1973.

Wolper, Stanley. *India*. Berkeley and Los Angeles, University of California Press, 1991.

—. *A New History of India*. New York, Oxford University Press, 1977, 3rd Ed., 1989.

Zimmer, Heinrich. *Philosophies of India*. Campbell, Joseph, Ed. Bollington Series 25. Princeton, New Jersey, Princeton University Press, 1969.

OFFICIAL DOCUMENTS

Government of India Tourist Promotion Book. "Heritage of Dance." April 1985.

India Tourism Development Corporation. "Come to the Buddha." Thomson Press Ltd., Faridabad, 1983.

"Population, Development and the Environment: An agenda for the 1990s," Proceedings of the National Conference of Non-Governmental Organizations. Bombay, Family Planning Association of India, April 14-16, 1991.

"The Life of the People of India," directed by Dr. Kumar Suresh Singh, New Delhi, ASI, Government of India, 1993.

MAGAZINES, JOURNALS, AND NEWSPAPERS

Alive, July 1989. Anuradha Paul. "Anatomy of Inimitable Art, Kathakali."

Femina, July 8, 1994. p. 34. Times of India Publication. "A Page out of the Miss Universe File." "Some thoughts penned down."

Frontline, Sept. 23, 1994. pp. 87-89. Tarun Chhabra. "Forgotten Culture: Todas, their life and times."

Illustrated Weekly of India, April 1993, "Death Wish."

Mid-Day, June 27, 1995. "Castles in the Air," p. A8 and "Playing House," p. A10.

Sanctuary Magazine, Vol. 10, No. 5, Sept/Oct. 1990. E. Narayanan "The Backwaters of Kerala."

Sunday Mid-Day, Variety, July 9, 1995. "Carry on Cleo."

Sunday Mid-Day, Part 2, July 2, 1995. pp. 2–3. "Pontiff of Peace."

The India Magazine, 1993. Vol. 14. p. 34. "Toda," Delta printing press.

The India Magazine, September 1993, p. 6-16, Tarun Chhabra. "A Journey to the Toda Afterworld."

Voyage, Vol. 1. No. 2. Parsiana Publications Pvt. Ltd., 1993.

REFERENCES

Pages 6–7. Shivanath Jha, "The gory Ganges: The holy river spawns death in Bihar," Times of India, February 18-March 6, 1993, p. 43.

Pages 44–45. "Training Modules For Incorporation Of Family Welfare Messages," by Prof. H. Simon and Shri B. B. L. Sharma, New Delhi: National Institute of Health and Family Welfare, 1990.

Pages 58–59. "Anatomy of the Inimitable Art: Kathakali," by Anuradha Paul, Alive magazine, July 1989, Published by Heritage of Dance, Government of India.

Page 63. New Delhi, Brijbasi Printers, 1989.

Pages 84–85. Michael Tobias, *Life Force: The World of Jainism*, Berkeley, California: Asian Humanities Press, 1991. See also, Tobias, *A Naked Man*, Fremont, California: Jain Publishing, 1994, and Tobias, "Ahimsa: Non-Violence" PBS KRMA Television Network, 1987 Denver, Colorado.

Pages 96–97. "Delhi most polluted city in India," by P. K. Surendran, *Times of India*, February 6, 1993, *Illustrated Weekly* of India, April 24-30, 1993.

Pages 104–105. *The Toda of South India: A New Look, by Anthony R. Walk*er, Delhi: Hindustan Publishing Corporation, 1986.

Pages 140–141. World Resources 1992-1993, A Report by The World Resources Institute, in collaboration with The United Nations Environment Programme and The United Nations Development Programme, New York: Oxford University Press, 1992.

Pages 166–167. Soutik Biswas, "Troubled Waters," *India Today*, February 28, 1993.

ABOVE:

Circular cottages at the *Nrityagram* Dance Village near Bangalore. Well-known exponents of classical Indian dance live here and teach their students the subtle and demanding techniques of ancient dance forms.

AVINASH PASRICHA